A TALK ON LANGUAGE.

The teacher is recommended, before assigning any lesson, to occupy the time of at least two or three recitations, in talking with his pupils about language, always remembering that, in order to secure the interest of his class, he must allow his pupils to take an active part in the exercise. The teacher should guide the thought of his class; but, if he attempt to do *all the talking*, he will find, when he concludes, that he has been left to do *all the thinking*.

We give below a few hints in conducting this talk on language, but the teacher is not expected to confine himself to them. He will, of course, be compelled, in some instances, to resort to various devices in order to obtain from the pupils answers equivalent to those here suggested.

LESSON 1.

+Teacher+.—I will pronounce these three sounds very slowly and distinctly, thus: *b-u-d*. Notice, it is the *power*, or *sound*, of the letter, and not its name, that I give. What did you hear?

+Pupil+.—I heard three sounds.

+T.—+Give them. I will write on the board, so that you can see them, three letters—*b-u-d*. Are these letters, taken separately, signs to you of anything?

+P.—+Yes, they are signs to me of the three sounds that I have just heard.

+T.—+What then do these letters, taken separately, picture to your eye?

+P.—+They picture the sounds that came to my ear.

+T+.—Letters then are the signs of what?

+P.—Letters are the signs of sounds+.

+T+.—I will pronounce the same three sounds more rapidly, uniting them more closely—*bud*. These sounds, so united, form a spoken word. Of what do you think when you hear the word *bud*?

+P+.—I think of a little round thing that grows to be a leafy branch or a flower.

+T+.—Did you see the thing when you were thinking of it?

+P+.—No.

+T+.—Then you must have had a picture of it in your mind. We call this +mental picture+ an +idea+. What called up this idea?

+P+.—It was called up by the word *bud,* which I heard.

+T+.—A *spoken word* then is the sign of what?

+P.—A spoken word is the sign of an idea+.

+T+.—I will call up the same idea in another way. I will *write* three *letters* and unite them thus: *bud.* What do you see?

+P+.—I see the word *bud.*

+T+.—If we call the other word *bud* a *spoken* word, what shall we call this?

+P+.—This is a *written* word.

+T+.—If they stand for the same idea, how do they differ?

+P+.—I *see* this, and I *heard* that.

+T+.—You will observe that we have called attention to *four* different things; viz., the +real bud+; your *mental picture* of the bud, which we have called an +idea+; and the +two words+, which we have called signs of this idea, the one addressed to the ear, and the other to the eye.

If the pupil be brought to see these distinctions, it may aid him to observe more closely and express himself more clearly.

LESSON 2.

+Teacher+.—What did you learn in the previous Lesson?

+Pupil+.—I learned that a spoken word is composed of certain sounds, and that letters are signs of sounds, and that spoken and written words are the signs of ideas.

This question should be passed from one pupil to another till all of these answers are elicited.

All the written words in all the English books ever made, are formed of twenty-six letters, representing about forty sounds. These letters and these sounds make up what is called artificial language.

Of these twenty-six letters, +a, e, i, o, u+, and sometimes +w+ and +y+, are called +vowels+, and the remainder are called +consonants+.

In order that you may understand what kind of sounds the vowels stand for, and what kinds the consonants represent, I will tell you something about the *human voice*.

The air breathed out from your lungs beats against two flat muscles, stretched like strings across the top of the windpipe, and causes them to vibrate. This vibrating makes sound. Take a thread, put one end between your teeth, hold the other in your fingers, draw it tight and strike it, and you will understand how voice is made.

If the voice thus produced comes out through the mouth held well open, a class of sounds is formed which we call *vowel* sounds.

But, if the voice is held back by your palate, tongue, teeth, or lips, *one* kind of *consonant* sounds is made. If the *breath* is driven out *without voice*, and is held back by these same parts of the mouth, the *other* kind of *consonant* sounds is formed. Ex. of both: *b, d, g; p, t, k.*

The teacher and pupils should practice on these sounds till the three kinds can easily be distinguished.

You are now prepared to understand what I mean when I say that the +vowels+ are the +letters+ which stand for the +open sounds of the voice+, and that the +consonants+ are the +letters+ which stand for the sounds made by the +obstructed voice+ and the +obstructed breath+.

The teacher can here profitably spend a few minutes in showing how ideas may be communicated by *Natural Language,* the language of *sighs, groans, gestures* of the hands, *attitudes* of the body, *expressions* of the face, *tones* of the voice, etc. He can show that, in conversation, we sometimes couple this *Natural Language* of *tone* and *gesture* with our language of words, in order to make a stronger impression. Let the pupil be told that, if the passage contain feeling, he should do the same in *Reading* and *Declaiming.*

Let the following definitions be learned, and given at the next recitation.

+DEFINITION.—Artificial Language, or *Language Proper,* consists of the spoken and written words used to communicate ideas and thoughts+.

+DEFINITION.—*English Grammar* is the science which teaches the forms, uses, and relations of the words of the English Language+.

LESSON 3

Let the pupils be required to tell what they learned in the previous lessons.

+Teacher+.—When I pronounce the two words *star* and *bud* thus: *star bud*, how many ideas, or mental pictures, do I call up to you?

+Pupil+.—Two.

+T+.—Do you see any connection between these ideas?

+P+.—No.

+T+.—When I utter the two words *bud* and *swelling*, thus: *bud swelling*, do you see any connection in the ideas they stand for?

+P+.—Yes, I imagine that I see a bud expanding, or growing larger.

+T+.—I will connect two words more closely, so as to express a thought: *Buds swell*. A thought has been formed in my mind when I say, *Buds swell*; and these two words, in which something is said of something else, express that thought, and make what we call a *sentence*. In the former expression, *bud swelling* it is assumed, or taken for granted, that buds perform the act; in the latter, the swelling is asserted as a fact.

Leaves falling. Do these two words express two ideas merely associated, or do they express a thought?

+P+.—They express ideas merely associated.

+T+.—*Leaves fall.*

Same question.

+P+.—A thought.

+T+.—Why?

+P+.—Because, in these words, there is something *said* or *asserted* of leaves.

+T+.—When I say, *Falling leaves rustle,* does *falling* tell what is thought of leaves?

+P+.—No.

+T+.—What does *falling* do?

+P+.—It tells the *kind* of leaves you are thinking and speaking of.

+T+.—What word *does* tell what is thought of leaves?

+P+.—*Rustle.*

+T+.—You see then that in the thought there are two parts; something of which we think, and that which we think about it.

Let the pupils give other examples.

LESSON 4.

Commit to memory all definitions.

+DEFINITION.—A *Sentence* is the expression of a thought in words+.

Which of the following expressions contain words that have *no connection*, which contain words *merely associated,* and which are *sentences*?

1. Flowers bloom. 2. Ice melts. 3. Bloom ice. 4. Grass grows. 5. Brooks babble. 6. Babbling brooks. 7. Grass soar. 8. Doors open. 9. Open doors. 10. Cows graze. 11. Curling smoke. 12. Sugar graze. 13. Dew sparkles. 14. Hissing serpents. 15. Smoke curls. 16. Serpents hiss. 17. Smoke curling. 18. Serpents sparkles. 19. Melting babble. 20. Eagles soar. 21. Birds chirping. 22. Birds are chirping. 23. Birds chirp. 24. Gentle cows. 25. Eagles are soaring. 26. Bees ice. 27. Working bees. 28. Bees work. 29. Crawling serpents. 30. Landscape piano. 31. Serpents crawl. 32. Eagles clock. 33. Serpents crawling.

LESSON 5.

Illustrate, by the use of *a*, *b*, and *p*, the difference between the *sounds* of letters and their *names*. Letters are the signs of what? What is an idea? A *spoken* word is the sign of what? A *written* word is the sign of what? How do they differ? To what four different things did we call attention in Lesson 1?

How are *vowel* sounds made? How are the two kinds of *consonant* sounds made? What are vowels? Name them. What are consonants? What is artificial language, or language proper? What do you understand by natural language? What is English grammar?

What three kinds of expressions are spoken of in Lessons 3 and 4? Give examples of each. What is a sentence?

LESSON 6.

ANALYSIS.

On the following sentences, let the pupils be exercised according to the model.

+Model+.—*Intemperance degrades*. Why is this a *sentence?* Ans.—Because it expresses a thought. Of what is something thought? Ans.—Intemperance. Which word tells what is thought? Ans.—*Degrades*.

1. Magnets attract. 2. Horses neigh. 3. Frogs leap. 4. Cold contracts. 5. Sunbeams dance. 6. Heat expands. 7. Sunlight gleams. 8. Banners wave. 9. Grass withers. 10. Sailors climb. 11. Rabbits burrow. 12. Spring advances.

You see that in these sentences there are two parts. The parts are the +Subject+ and the +Predicate+.

+DEFINITION.—The *Subject of a sentence* names that of which something is thought+.

+DEFINITION.—The *Predicate of a sentence* tells what is thought+.

+DEFINITION.—The *Analysis of a sentence* is the separation of it into its parts+.

Analyze, according to the model, the following sentences.

+Model+.—*Stars twinkle*. This is a *sentence*, because it expresses a thought. *Stars* is the *subject*, because it names that of which something is thought; *twinkle* is the *predicate*, because it tells what is thought.

+To the Teacher+.—After the pupils become familiar with the definitions, the "Models" may be varied, and some of the reasons maybe made specific; as, "*Plants* names the things we tell about; *droop* tells what plants do," etc.

Guard against needless repetition.

1. Plants droop. 2. Books help. 3. Clouds float. 4. Exercise strengthens. 5. Rain falls. 6. Time flies. 7. Rowdies fight. 8. Bread nourishes. 9. Boats capsize. 10. Water flows. 11. Students learn. 12. Horses gallop.

LESSON 7.

ANALYSIS AND THE DIAGRAM.

+Hints for Oral Instruction+.—I will draw on the board a heavy, or shaded, line, and divide it into two parts, thus:

```
          |
==========|============
     |
```

We will consider the first part as the sign of the *subject* of a sentence, and the second part as the sign of the *predicate* of a sentence.

Now, if I write a word over the first line, thus—(doing it)—you will understand that that word is the subject of a sentence. If I write a word over the second line, thus—you will understand that that word is the predicate of a sentence.

```
    Planets | revolve
============|===========
      |
```

The class can see by this picture that *Planets revolve* is a sentence, that *planets* is the subject, and that *revolve* is the predicate.

These signs, or illustrations, made up of straight lines, we call +Diagrams+.

+DEFINITION.—A *Diagram* is a picture of the offices and relations of the different parts of a sentence+.

Analyze and *diagram* the following sentences.

1. Waves dash. 2. Kings reign. 3. Fruit ripens. 4. Stars shine. 5. Steel tarnishes. 6. Insects buzz. 7. Paul preached. 8. Poets sing. 9. Nero fiddled. 10. Larks sing. 11. Water ripples. 12. Lambs frisk. 13. Lions roar. 14. Tigers growl. 15. Breezes sigh. 16. Carthage fell. 17. Morning dawns. 18. Showers descended. 19. Diamonds sparkle. 20. Alexander conquered. 21. Jupiter thunders. 22. Columbus sailed, 23. Grammarians differ. 24. Cornwallis surrendered.

* * * * *

LESSON 8.

SENTENCE-BUILDING.

You have now learned to analyze sentences, that is, to separate them into their parts. You must next learn to put these parts together, that is, to *build sentences.*

We will find one part, and you must find the other and do the building.

+To the Teacher+.—Let some of the pupils write their sentences on the board, while others are reading theirs. Then let the work on the board be corrected.

Correct any expression that does not make *good sense,* or that asserts something not strictly true; for the pupil should early be taught to *think accurately*, as well as to write and speak grammatically.

Correct all mistakes in *spelling,* and in the use of *capital letters* and the *period.*

Call attention to the agreement in form of the predicate with the subject. See Notes, p. 163.

Insist on neatness. Collect the papers before the recitation closes.

+CAPITAL LETTER-RULE.—The first word of every sentence must begin with a *capital letter+.*

+PERIOD—RULE.—A *period* must be placed after every sentence that simply affirms, denies, or expresses a command+.

Construct sentences by supplying a *subject* to each of the following *predicates.*

Ask yourself the question, What swim, sink, hunt, etc.?

1. —— swim. 2. —— sinks. 3. —— hunt. 4. —— skate. 5. —— jingle. 6. —— decay. 7. —— climb. 8. —— creep. 9. —— run. 10. —— walk. 11. —— snort. 12. —— kick. 13. —— flashes. 14. —— flutters. 15. —— paddle. 16. —— toil. 17. —— terrifies. 18. —— rages. 19. —— expand. 20. —— jump. 21. —— hop. 22. —— bellow. 23. —— burns. 24. —— evaporates.

This exercise may profitably be extended by requiring the pupils to supply *several* subjects to each predicate.

LESSON 9.

SENTENCE-BUILDING—Continued.

Construct sentences by supplying a *predicate* to each of the following *subjects*.

Ask yourself the question, Artists do what?

1. Artists ——. 2. Sailors ——. 3. Tides ——. 4. Whales ——. 5. Gentlemen ——. 6. Swine ——. 7. Clouds ——. 8. Girls ——. 9. Fruit ——. 10. Powder ——. 11. Hail ——. 12. Foxes ——. 13. Water ——. 14. Frost ——. 15. Man ——. 16. Blood ——. 17. Kings ——. 18. Lilies ——. 19. Roses ——. 20. Wheels ——. 21. Waves ——. 22. Dew ——. 23. Boys ——. 24. Volcanoes ——. 25. Storms ——. 26. Politicians ——. 27. Serpents ——. 28. Chimneys ——. 29. Owls ——. 30. Rivers ——. 31. Nations ——. 32. Indians ——. 33. Grain ——. 34. Rogues ——. 34. Volcanoes ——. 35. Rome ——. 36. Briars ——.

This exercise may be extended by requiring the pupils to supply several predicates to each subject.

LESSON 10.

REVIEW QUESTIONS.

Of what two parts does a sentence consist? What is the subject of a sentence? What is the predicate of a sentence? What is the analysis of a sentence?

What is a diagram? What rule for the use of capital letters have you learned? What rule for the period?

Impromptu Exercise.

Let the pupils "choose sides," as in a spelling match. Let the teacher select *predicates* from Lesson 8, and give them alternately to the pupils thus arranged. The first pupil prefixes to his word whatever suitable subjects he can think of, the teacher judging of their fitness and keeping the count. This pupil now rises and remains standing until some one else, on his side or the other, shall have prefixed to his word a greater number of apt subjects. The strife is to see who shall be standing at the close of the match, and which side shall have furnished the greater number of subjects. The exercise may be continued with the *subjects* of Lesson 9. Each pupil is to be limited to the same time—one or two minutes.

LESSON 11.

The +*predicate*+ sometimes contains +*more than one word*+.

Analyze and *diagram* according to the model.

+Model+.—*Socrates was poisoned.*

Socrates | was poisoned
============|================
   |

This is a sentence, because it expresses a thought. *Socrates* is the subject, because ——; *was poisoned* is the predicate, because ——. [Footnote: The word *because*—suggesting a reason—should be dropped from these "+Models+" whenever it may lead to mere mechanical repetition.]

1. Napoleon was banished. 2. Andre was captured. 3. Money is circulated. 4. Columbus was imprisoned. 5. Acorns are sprouting. 6. Bells are tolled. 7. Summer has come. 8. Sentences may be analyzed. 9. Clouds are reddening. 10. Air may be weighed. 11. Jehovah shall reign. 12. Corn is planted. 13. Grammarians will differ. 14. Snow is falling. 15. Leaves are rustling. 16. Children will prattle. 17. Crickets are chirping. 18. Eclipses have been foretold. 19. Storms may abate. 20. Deception may have been

practiced. 21. Esau was hated. 22. Treason should have been punished. 23. Bees are humming. 24. Sodom might have been spared.

LESSON 12.

SENTENCE-BUILDING.

+To the Teacher+.—Continue oral and written exercises in agreement. See
Notes, pp. 163,164.

Prefix the little helping words in the *second column* to such of the more important words in the *third column* as with them will make complete predicates, and join these predicates to all subjects in the *first column* with which they will unite to make good sense.

    1 | 2 | 3

Burgoyne | are | woven.
Henry Hudson | was | defeated.
Sparrows | can be | condensed.
Comets | is | inhaled.
Time | have been | worn.
Turbans | may be | slacked.
Lime | has been | wasted.
Steam | could have been | seen.
Air | must have been | deceived.
Carpets | were | quarreling.

LESSON 13.

Point out the *subject* and the predicate of each sentence in Lessons 28, 31, 34.

Look first for the word that asserts, and then, by putting *who* or *what* before this *predicate*, the *subject* may easily be found.

+To the Teacher+.—Most violations of the rules of concord come from a failure to recognize the relation of subject and predicate when these parts are transposed or are separated by other words. Such constructions should therefore receive special attention. See Notes, pp. 164, 165.

Introduce the class to the Parts of Speech before the close of this recitation. See "Hints for Oral Instruction."

See "Suggestions for COMPOSITION EXERCISES," p. 8, last paragraph.

LESSON 14.

+Hints for Oral Instruction+.—By the assistance of the few hints here given, the ingenious teacher may render this usually dry subject interesting and highly attractive. By questioning the pupil as to what he has seen and heard, his interest may be excited and his curiosity awakened.

Suppose that we make an imaginary excursion to some pleasant field or grove, where we may study the habits, the plumage, and the songs of the little birds.

If we attempt to make the acquaintance of every little feathered singer we meet, we shall never get to the end of our pleasant task: but we find that some resemble one another in size, shape, color, habits, and song. These we associate together and call them sparrows.

We find others differing essentially from the sparrows, but resembling one another. These we call robins.

We thus find that, although we were unable to become acquainted with each *individual* bird, they all belong to a few *classes*, with which we may soon become familiar.

It is so with the words of our language. There are many thousand words, all of which belong to eight classes.

These classes of words are called +Parts of Speech+.

We classify birds according to their form, color, etc., but we group words into *classes*, called +Parts of Speech+, with respect to their use in the *sentence*.

We find that many words are names. These we put in one class and call them
+Nouns+.

Each pupil may give the name of something in the room; the name of a distinguished person; a name that may be applied to a class of persons; the name of an animal; the name of a place: the name of a river; the name of a mountain; the name of something which we cannot see or touch, but of which we can think; as, *beauty, mind*.

Remind the pupils frequently that these *names* are all *nouns*.

NOUNS.

+DEFINITION.—A *Noun* is the name of anything+.

Write in columns, headed *nouns*, the names of domestic animals, of garden vegetables, of flowers, of trees, of articles sold in a dry goods store, and of things that cannot be seen or touched; as, *virtue, time, life*.

Write and arrange, according to the following model, the names of things that can *float, fly, walk, work, sit*, or *sing*.

Nouns.

Cork |

Clouds |

+Model+.—Wood + floats or float.

Ships |

Boys |

Such expressions as *Cork floats* are *sentences*, and the nouns *cork, ship,* etc., are the subjects. You will find that *+every subject+ is a +noun+ or some word or words used for a noun.*

Be prepared to analyze and parse the sentences which you have made. *Naming the class to which a word belongs is the first step in parsing.*

+Model for Analysis+.—This is a sentence, because ———-; *cork* is the subject, because ———-; *floats* is the predicate, because ———-.

+Parsing+.—*Cork* is a *noun,* because it is the name of a thing—the bark of a tree.

LESSON 15.

Select and write all the nouns in the sentences given in Lessons 28, 31, 34.

Tell why they are nouns.

In writing the nouns, observe the following rule.

+CAPITAL LETTER—RULE.—Every proper or individual name must begin with a capital letter+.

+To the Teacher+.—See Notes, pp. 167-169.

REVIEW QUESTIONS.

With respect to what, do we classify words (Lesson 14)? What are such classes called? Can you illustrate this classification? What are all names? What is a noun? What is the first step in parsing? What is the rule for writing individual names?

LESSON 22.

ADJECTIVES.

+Hints for Oral Instruction+.—You are now prepared to consider the *fourth part of speech*. Those words that are added to the subject to modify its meaning are called +Adjectives+.

Some grammarians have formed a separate class of the little words *the*, and *an* or *a*, calling them *articles*.

I will write the word *boys* on the board, and you may name adjectives that will appropriately modify it. As you give them, *I* will write these adjectives in a column.

Adjectives.

small | large | white | black | straight + boys. crooked | five | some | all |

What words here modify *boys* by adding the idea of size? What by adding the idea of color? What by adding the idea of form? What by adding the idea of number? What are such words called? Why?

Let the teacher name familiar objects and require the pupils to join appropriate adjectives to the names till their stock is exhausted.

+DEFINITION.—An *Adjective* is a word used to modify a noun or a pronoun+.

Analysis and Parsing.

+Model+.—*A fearful storm was raging.* Diagram and analyze as in Lesson 20.

+Written Parsing+.

Nouns. | *Pronouns.* | *Adjectives.* | *Verbs.* storm | —— | A fearful | was raging.

+Oral Parsing+.—*A* is an *adjective*, because it is joined to the noun *storm*, to modify its meaning; *fearful* is an *adjective*, because ———; *storm* is a noun, because ———; *was raging* is a verb, because ———-.

1. The rosy morn advances. 2. The humble boon was obtained. 3. An unyielding firmness was displayed. 4. The whole earth smiles. 5. Several subsequent voyages were made. 6. That burly mastiff must be secured. 7. The slender greyhound was released. 8. The cold November rain is falling. 9. That valuable English watch has been sold. 10. I alone have escaped. 11. Both positions can be defended. 12. All such discussions should have been avoided. 13. That dilapidated old wooden building has fallen.

+To the Teacher+.—See Notes, pp. 169, 170.

LESSON 23.

SENTENCE-BUILDING.

Prefix five adjectives to each of the following nouns.

Shrubs, wilderness, beggar, cattle, cloud.

Write ten sentences with modified subjects, using in each two or more of the following adjectives.

A, an, the, heroic, one, all, many, every, either, first, tenth, frugal, great, good, wise, honest, immense, square, circular, oblong, oval, mild, virtuous, universal, sweet, careless, fragrant.

Write five sentences with modified subjects, each of which shall contain one of the following words as a subject.

Chimney, hay, coach, robber, horizon.

An and *a* are forms of the same word, once spelled *an*, and meaning *one*. After losing something of this force, *an* was still used before vowels and consonants alike; as, *an eagle, an ball, an hair, an use*. Still later, and for the sake of ease in speaking, the word came to have the two forms mentioned above; and an was retained before letters having vowel sounds, but it dropped its *n* and became *a* before letters having consonant sounds. This is the present usage.

CORRECT THESE ERRORS.

A apple; a obedient child; an brickbat; an busy boy.

CORRECT THESE ERRORS.

A heir; a hour; a honor.

Notice, the first letter of these words is *silent*.

CORRECT THESE ERRORS.

An unit; an utensil; an university; an ewe; an ewer; an union; an use; an history; an one.

Unit begins with the sound of the consonant *y*; and *one*, with that of *w*.

+To the Teacher+.—See "Suggestions for COMPOSITION EXERCISES," p. 8, last paragraph.

LESSON 24.

MODIFIED PREDICATES.

+Hints for Oral Instruction+.—I will now show you how the *predicate* of a sentence may be modified.

The ship sails gracefully. What word is here joined to *sails* to tell the *manner* of sailing? +P+.—*Gracefully*.

+T+.—*The ship sails immediately*. What word is here joined to *sails* to tell the *time* of sailing? +P+.—*Immediately*.

+T+.—*The, ship sails homeward*. What word is here joined to *sails* to tell the *direction* of sailing? +P+.—*Homeward*.

+T+.—These words *gracefully, immediately,* and *homeward* are modifiers of the predicate. In the first sentence, *sails gracefully* is the +Modified Predicate+.

Let the following modifiers be written on the board as the pupil suggests them.

    | instantly.
   | soon.
   | daily.

| hither.

The ship sails + hence.

| there.

| rapidly.

| smoothly.

| well.

Which words indicate the time of sailing? Which, the place? Which, the manner?

The teacher may suggest predicates, and require the pupils to find as many appropriate modifiers as they can.

The Predicate with its modifiers is called the +*Modified Predicate*+.

Analysis and Parsing.

Analyze and diagram the following sentences, and parse the nouns, pronouns, verbs, and adjectives.

+Model+.—*The letters were rudely carved.*

    letters | were carved
========|===============
\The | \rudely

+Written Parsing+.—See *Model*, Lesson 22.

+Oral Analysis+.—This is a sentence, because——; *letters* is the subject, because——; *were carved* is the predicate, because——; *The* is a modifier of the subject, because——; *rudely* is a modifier of the predicate, because

——; *The letters* is the modified subject, *were rudely carved* is the *modified predicate.*

1. He spoke eloquently. 2. She chattered incessantly. 3. They searched everywhere. 4. I shall know presently. 5. The bobolink sings joyously. 6. The crowd cheered heartily. 7. A great victory was finally won. 8. Threatening clouds are moving slowly. 9. The deafening waves dash angrily. 10. These questions may be settled peaceably. 11. The wounded soldier fought bravely. 12. The ranks were quickly broken. 13. The south wind blows softly. 14. Times will surely change. 15. An hour stole on.

LESSON 25.

ONE MODIFIER JOINED TO ANOTHER.

Analyze and diagram the following sentences, and parse the nouns, pronouns, adjectives, and verbs.

+Model+.—*The frightened animal fled still more rapidly.*

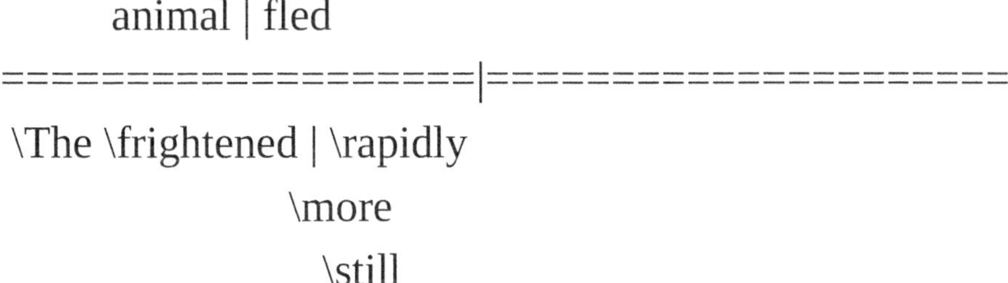

+Explanation of the Diagram+.—Notice that the three lines forming this group all slant the same way to show that each stands for a modifying word. The line standing for the principal word of the group is joined to the predicate line. The end of each of the other two lines is broken, and turned to touch its principal at an angle.

+Oral Analysis+.—This is a sentence, because——; *animal* is the subject, because——; *fled* is the predicate, because——; *The* and *frightened* are modifiers of the subject, because——; *still more rapidly* is a modifier of the predicate, because it is a group of words joined to it to limit its meaning; *rapidly* is the principal word of the group; *more* modifies *rapidly*, and *still* modifies *more, The frightened animal* is the modified subject; *fled still more rapidly* is the modified predicate.

1. The crocus flowers very early. 2. A violet bed is budding near. 3. The Quakers were most shamefully persecuted. 4. Perhaps he will return. 5. We laughed very heartily. 6. The yellow poplar leaves floated down. 7. The wind sighs so mournfully. 8. Few men have ever fought so stubbornly. 9. The debt will probably be paid. 10. The visitor will soon be here. 11. That humane project was quite generously sustained. 12. A perfectly innocent man was very cruelly persecuted.

REVIEW QUESTIONS.

What is an adjective? What are the words *an* or *a,* and *the* called by some grammarians? When is *a* used, and when *an?* Give examples of their misuse.

What is the modified predicate? Give an example. Give an example of one modifier joined to another.

LESSON 26.

Select your subjects from Lesson 9, and construct twenty sentences having modified subjects and modified predicates.

Impromptu Exercise.

Select sentences from Lessons 6, 7, and 11, and conduct the exercise as directed in Lesson 10. Let the strife be to see who can supply the greatest number of modifiers to the subject and to the predicate. The teacher can vary this exercise.

LESSON 27.

ADVERBS.

+Hints for Oral Instruction+.—You have learned, in the preceding Lessons, that the meaning of the predicate may be limited by modifiers, and that one modifier may be joined to another. Words used to modify the predicate of a sentence and those used to modify modifiers belong to one class, or one *part of speech*, and are called +Adverbs+.

+T+.—*She decided too hastily*. What word tells how she decided? +P+.—-*Hastily*. +T+.—What word tells how hastily? +P+.—*Too*. +T+.—What then are the words *too* and *hastily?* +P+.—Adverbs.

+T+.—*Too much time has been wasted*. What word modifies *much* by telling how much? +P+.—*Too*. +T+.—What *part of speech* is *much?* +P+. —An adjective. +T+.—What then is *too?* +P+.—An adverb.

+T+.—Why is *too* in the first sentence an adverb? Why is *too* in the second sentence an adverb? Why is *hastily* an adverb?

Let the teacher use the following and similar examples, and continue the questions. *He thinks so. So much time has been wasted.*

Let the teacher give verbs, adjectives, and adverbs, and require the pupils to modify them by appropriate adverbs.

+DEFINITION.—*An Adverb* is a word used to modify a verb, an adjective, or an adverb+.

Analysis and Parsing.

Analyze, diagram, and parse the following sentences.

+Model+.—*We have been very agreeably disappointed.* +Diagram+ as in.
Lesson 25.

For +Written Parsing+, use *Model,* Lesson 22, adding a column for adverbs.

+Oral Parsing+.—*We* is a pronoun, because——; *have been disappointed* is a verb, because——; *very* is an *adverb,* because it is joined to the adverb *agreeably* to tell how agreeably; *agreeably* is an *adverb,* because it is joined to the verb *have been disappointed* to indicate manner.

1. The plough-boy plods homeward. 2. The water gushed forth. 3. Too much time was wasted. 4. She decided too hastily. 5. You should listen more attentively. 6. More difficult sentences must be built. 7. An intensely painful operation was performed. 8. The patient suffered intensely. 9. That story was peculiarly told. 10. A peculiarly interesting story was told. 11. An extravagantly high price was paid. 12. That lady dresses extravagantly.

The pupil will notice that, in some of the examples above, the same adverb modifies an adjective in one sentence and an adverb in another, and that, in other examples, an adjective and a verb are modified by the same word. You may learn from this why such modifiers are grouped into one class.

LESSON 28.

ANALYSIS AND PARSING.

MISCELLANEOUS EXAMPLES FOR REVIEW.

1. You must diagram neatly. 2. The sheaves are nearly gathered. 3. The wheat is duly garnered. 4. The fairies were called together. 5. The birds chirp merrily. 6. This reckless adventurer has returned. 7. The wild woods rang. 8. White fleecy clouds are floating above. 9. Those severe laws have been repealed. 10. A republican government was established. 11. An unusually large crop had just been harvested. 12. She had been waiting quite patiently. 13. A season so extremely warm had never before been known. 14. So brave a deed [Footnote: *Can be commended* is the verb, and *not* is an adverb.] cannot be too warmly commended.

LESSON 29.

SENTENCE-BUILDING.

MISCELLANEOUS EXERCISES FOR REVIEW.

Build sentences containing the following adverbs.

Hurriedly, solemnly, lightly, well, how, somewhere, abroad, forever, seldom, exceedingly.

Using the following subjects and predicates as foundations, build six sentences having modified subjects and modified predicates, two of which shall contain adverbs modifying adjectives; two, adverbs modifying adverbs; and two, adverbs modifying verbs.

1. ———- boat glides ——-. 2. ———- cloud is rising ——-. 3. ———- breezes are blowing ——-. 4. ———- elephant was captured ——-. 5. ———- streams flow ——-. 6. ———- spring has opened ——-.

We here give you, in classes, the material out of which you are to build five sentences with modified subjects and modified predicates.

Select the subject and the predicate first.

Nouns and Pronouns. Verbs. Adjectives. Adverbs.

branch | was running | large, that | lustily coach | were played | both, the | downward they | cried | all, an | very we | is growing | several, a | rapidly games | cheered | amusing | not, loudly, then

LESSON 30.

ERRORS FOR CORRECTION.

+To the Teacher+.—We here suggest additional work in composition, with particular reference to the choice and position of adjectives. See Notes, pp. 171,172.

+*Caution*+.—When two or more adjectives are used with a noun, care must be taken in their arrangement. If there is any difference in their relative importance, place nearest the noun the one that is most intimately connected with it.

+To the Teacher+.—We have in mind here those numerous cases where one adjective modifies the noun, and the second modifies the noun as limited by the first. *All ripe apples are picked*. Here *ripe* modifies *apples*, but *all* modifies *apples* limited by *ripe*. Not *all apples* are *picked*, but only *all* that are *ripe*.

CORRECT THE FOLLOWING ERRORS OF POSITION.

A wooden pretty bowl stood on the table.
The blue beautiful sky is cloudless.
A young industrious man was hired.
The new marble large house was sold.

+*Caution*+.—When the adjectives are of the *same* rank, place them where they will sound the best. This will usually be in the order of their length—the longest last.

CORRECT THESE ERRORS.

An entertaining and fluent speaker followed.
An enthusiastic, noisy, large crowd was addressed.

+*Caution*+.—Do not use the pronoun +*them*+ for the adjective +*those*+.

CORRECT THESE ERRORS.

Them books are nicely bound.
Them two sentences should be corrected.

CORRECT THE FOLLOWING MISCELLANEOUS ERRORS.

arouse, o romans
hear, o israel
it is i
i may be Mistaken
you Have frequently been warned
some Very savage beasts have been Tamed

REVIEW QUESTIONS.

What is an adverb? Give an example of an adverb modifying an adjective; one modifying a verb; one modifying an adverb. Why are such expressions as *a wooden pretty bowl* faulty? Why is *an enthusiastic, noisy, large crowd* faulty? Why is *them books* wrong? Why is *i may be Mistaken* wrong? Why is *hear, o israel,* wrong? Study the Review Questions given in previous Lessons.

+To the Teacher+.—See COMPOSITION EXERCISES in the Supplement—Selection from Darwin.

LESSON 31.

PHRASES INTRODUCED BY PREPOSITIONS.

+Hints for Oral Instruction+.—In the preceding Lessons, you have learned that several words may be grouped together and used as one modifier. In the examples given, the principal word is joined directly to the subject or to the predicate, and this word is modified by another word. In this Lesson also groups of words are used as modifiers, but these words are not united with one another, or with the word which the group modifies, just as they are in the preceding Lessons. I will write on the board this sentence: *De Soto marched into Florida.* +T+.—What tells where De Soto marched? +P+.—*Into Florida.* +T+.—What is the principal word of the group? +P+.—*Florida.* +T+.—Is *Florida* joined directly to the predicate, as rapidly was in Lesson 25? +P+.—No. +T+.—What little word comes in to unite the modifier to *marched?* +P+.—*Into.* +T+.—Does *Florida* alone, tell where he marched? +P+.—No. +T+.—Does *into* alone, tell where he marched? +P+.—No.

+T+.—These groups of related words are called +Phrases+. Let the teacher draw on the board the diagram of the sentence above.

Phrases of the form illustrated in this diagram are the most common, and they perform a very important function in our language.

Let the teacher frequently call attention to the fact that all the words of a phrase are *taken together* to perform *one distinct office.*

A phrase modifying the subject is equivalent to an adjective, and, frequently, may be changed into one. *The dew of the morning has passed away.* What word may be used for the phrase *of the morning?* +P+.—*Morning.* +T+.—Yes. The *morning* dew has passed away.

A phrase modifying the predicate is equivalent to an adverb, and, frequently, may be changed into one. *We shall go to that place.* What word may be used for the phrase, *to that place?* +P+.—*There.* +T+.—Yes. We shall go *there.*

Change the phrases in these sentences:—-

_A citizen of America was insulted.

We walked toward home_.

Let the teacher write on the board the following words, and require the pupils to add to each, one or more words to complete a phrase, and then to construct a sentence in which the phrase may be properly employed: *To, from, by, at, on, with, in, into, over.*

+DEFINITION.—A *Phrase* is a group of words denoting related ideas but not expressing a thought+.

Analysis and Parsing.

Analyze the following sentences, and parse the nouns, pronouns, adjectives, verbs, and adverbs.

Model.—*The finest trout in the lake are generally caught in the deepest water.*

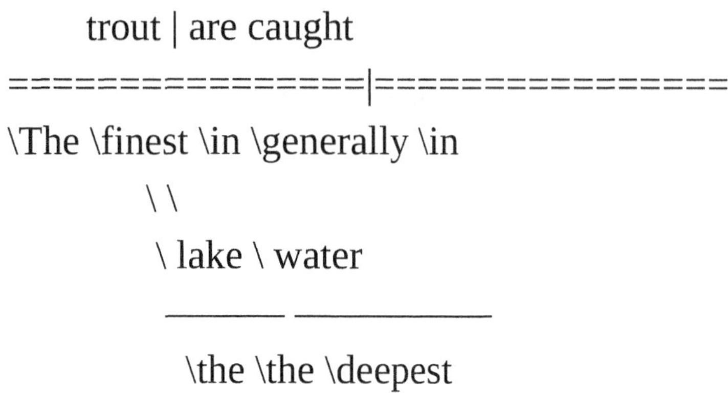

+Explanation of the Diagram+.—You will notice that the diagram of the *phrase* is made up of a slanting line, standing for the introductory and connecting word, and a horizontal line, representing the principal word. Under the latter, are placed the little slanting lines standing for the modifiers of the principal word. Here and elsewhere all modifiers are joined to their principal words by slanting lines.

+Oral Analysis+.—This is a sentence, because ———; *trout* is the subject, because ——-; *are caught* is the predicate, because ———; the words *The* and *finest*, and the phrase, *in the lake*, are modifiers of the subject, because ——-; the word *generally* and the phrase, *in the deepest water*, are modifiers of the predicate, because ———; *in* introduces the first phrase, and *lake* is the principal word; *in* introduces the second phrase, and *water* is the principal word; *the* and *deepest* are modifiers of *water*; *The finest trout in the lake* is the modified subject, and *are generally caught in the deepest water* is the modified predicate.

1. The gorilla lives in Africa. 2. It seldom rains in Egypt. 3. The Pilgrims landed at Plymouth. 4. The wet grass sparkled in the light. 5. The little brook ran swiftly under the bridge. 6. Burgoyne surrendered at Saratoga. 7. The steeples of the village pierced through the dense fog. 8. The gloom of

winter settled down on everything. 9. A gentle breeze blows from the south. 10. The temple of Solomon was destroyed. 11. The top of the mountain is covered with snow. 12. The second Continental Congress convened at Philadelphia.

LESSON 32.

SENTENCE-BUILDING.

Build sentences, employing the following phrases as modifiers.

To Europe, of oak, from Albany, at the station, through the fields, for vacation, among the Indians, of the United States.

Supply to the following predicates subjects modified by phrases.

—— is situated on the Thames. —— has arrived. —— was destroyed by an earthquake. —— was received. —— has just been completed. —— may be enjoyed.

Supply to the following subjects predicates modified by phrases.

Iron ——.
The trees ——.
Squirrels ——.
The Bible ——.
Sugar ——.
Cheese ——.
Paul ——.
Strawberries ——.
The mountain ——.

Write five sentences, each of which shall contain one or more phrases used as modifiers.

LESSON 33.

SENTENCE-BUILDING.

Re-write the following sentences, changing the italicized words into equivalent phrases.

+Model+.—A *golden* image was made.
An image *of gold* was made.

You will notice that the adjective *golden* was placed before the subject, but, when changed to a phrase, it followed the subject.

1. The book was *carefully* read. 2. The old soldiers fought *courageously*. 3. A group of children were strolling *homeward*. 4. No season of life should be spent *idly*. 5. The *English* ambassador has just arrived. 6. That *generous* act was liberally rewarded.

Change the following adjectives and adverbs into equivalent phrases, and employ the phrases in sentences of your own building.

Wooden, penniless, eastward, somewhere, here, evening, everywhere, yonder, joyfully, wintry.

Make a sentence out of the words in each line below.

Boat, waves, glides, the, the, over.

He, Sunday, church, goes, the, on, to.

Year, night, is dying, the, the, in.

Qualities, Charlemagne, vices, were alloyed, the, great, of, with.

Indians, America, intemperance, are thinned, the, out, of, by.

LESSON 34.

PREPOSITIONS.

+Hints for Oral Instruction+.—In the preceding Lessons, the little words that were placed before nouns, thus forming phrases, belong to a, class of words called +Prepositions+. You noticed that these words, which you have now learned to call prepositions, served to introduce phrases. The preposition shows the relation of the *idea* expressed by the principal word of the phrase to that of the word which the phrase modifies. It serves also to connect these words.

In the sentence, *The squirrel ran up a tree*, what word shows the relation of the act of running, to the tree? Ans. *Up*.

Other words may be used to express different relations. Repeat, nine times, the sentence above given, supplying, in the place of *up*, each of the following prepositions: *Around, behind, down, into, over, through, to, under, from*.

Let this exercise be continued, using such sentences as, *The man went into the house; The ship sailed toward the bay*.

+DEFINITION.—A *Preposition* is a word that introduces a phrase modifier, and shows the relation, in sense, of its principal word to the word modified+.

+Analysis and Parsing+.

+Model+.—*Flowers preach to us.*

For +Analysis+ and +Diagram+, see Lesson 31.

For +Written Parsing+, see Lesson 22. Add the needed columns.

+Oral Parsing+.—*Flowers* is a noun, because——; *preach* is a verb, because——; *to* is a *preposition*, because it shows the relation, in sense, between *us* and *preach; us* is a pronoun, because it is used instead of the name of the speaker and the names of those for whom he speaks.

1. The golden lines of sunset glow. 2. A smiling landscape lay before us. 3. Columbus was born at Genoa. 4. The forces of Hannibal were routed by Scipio. 5. The capital of New York is on the Hudson. 6. The ships sail over the boisterous sea. 7. All names of the Deity should begin with capital letters. 8. Air is composed chiefly of two invisible gases. 9. The greater portion of South America lies between the tropics. 10. The laurels of the warrior must at all times be dyed in blood. 11. The first word of every entire sentence should begin with a capital letter. 12. The subject of a sentence is generally placed before the predicate.

Impromptu Exercise.

(The teacher may find it profitable to make a separate lesson of this exercise.)

Let the teacher write on the board a subject and a predicate that will admit of many modifiers. The pupils are to expand the sentence into as many separate sentences as possible, each containing one apt phrase modifier. The competition is to see who can build the most and the best sentences in a given time. The teacher gathers up the slates and reads the work aloud, or has the pupils exchange slates and read it themselves.

LESSON 35.

COMPOUND SUBJECT AND COMPOUND PREDICATE.

When two or more subjects united by a connecting word have the same predicate, they form a +*Compound Subject;*+ and, when two or more predicates connected in like manner have the same subject, they form a +*Compound Predicate*+.

In the sentence, *Birds and bees can fly*, the two words *birds* and *bees*, connected by *and*, have the same predicate; the same action is asserted of both birds and bees. In the sentence, *Leaves fade and fall*, two assertions are made of the same things. In the first sentence, *birds* and *bees* form the *compound subject*; and, in the second, *fade* and *fall* form the *compound predicate*.

Analyze and parse the following sentences.

+Models+.—*Napoleon rose, reigned, and fell.*

Frogs, antelopes, and kangaroos can jump.

```
            rose Frogs
        ,=,===== ======.=.
         / ' ' \
Napoleon| / X ' reigned antelopes ' X \ | can jump
```

```
========|==| '======== ==========' |==|=========
    | \and' 'and/ |
       \ ' fell kangaroos ' /
         `_'====== ==========='='
```

+Explanation of the Diagram+.—The short line following the subject line represents the entire predicate, and is supposed to be continued in the three horizontal lines that follow, each of which represents one of the parts of the *compound predicate*. These three lines are united by dotted lines, which stand for the connecting words. The +X+ denotes that an *and* is understood.

Study this explanation carefully, and you will understand the other diagram.

+Oral Analysis+ of the first sentence.

This is a sentence, because ——; *Napoleon* is the subject, because ——; *rose, reigned*, and *fell* form the *compound predicate*, because they belong in common to the same subject, and say something about Napoleon. *And* connects *reigned* and *fell*.

1. The Rhine and the Rhone rise in Switzerland. 2. Time and tide wait for no man. 3. Washington and Lafayette fought for American Independence. 4. Wild birds shrieked, and fluttered on the ground. 5. The mob raged and roared. 6. The seasons came and went. 7. Pride, poverty, and fashion cannot live in the same house. 8. The tables of stone were cast to the ground and broken. 9. Silver or gold will be received in payment. 10. Days, months, years, and ages will circle away.

REVIEW QUESTIONS.

What is a phrase? A phrase modifying a subject is equivalent to what? Illustrate. A phrase modifying a predicate is equivalent to what? Illustrate.

What are prepositions? What do you understand by a compound subject? Illustrate. What do you understand by a compound predicate? Illustrate.

LESSON 36.

CONJUNCTIONS AND INTERJECTIONS.

The words *and* and *or,* used in the preceding Lesson to connect the nouns and the verbs, belong to a class of words called +*Conjunctions*+.

Conjunctions may also connect *words* used as *modifiers;* as,

A daring *but* foolish feat was performed.

They may connect phrases; as,

We shall go to Saratoga *and* to Niagara.

They may connect *clauses,* that is, expressions that, standing alone, would be sentences; as,

He must increase, *but* I must decrease.

+DEFINITION.—A *Conjunction,* is a word used to connect words, phrases, or clauses+.

The +*Interjection*+ is the eighth and last *part of speech.* Interjections are mere exclamations, and are without grammatical relation to any other word in the sentence.

+DEFINITION.—An *Interjection* is a word used to express strong or sudden feeling+.

Examples:—

Bravo! hurrah! pish! hush! ha, ha! alas! hail! lo! pshaw!

Analyze and parse the following sentences.

+Model+.—*Hurrah! that cool and fearless fireman has rushed into the house and up the burning stairs.*

```
   Hurrah
  ________


   fireman | has rushed
==================|=======================
\That\ and \ | \ and \
   \.....\ \........\
    \ \ \ \up
     \cool \fearless \into \stairs
                \ ____________
                \house \the \burning
                 ________
                    \the
```

+Explanation of the Diagram+.—The line representing the interjection is not connected with the diagram. Notice the dotted lines, one standing for the *and* which connects the two *word* modifiers; the other, for the *and* connecting the two *phrase* modifiers.

+Written Parsing+.

N. Pro. Adj. Vb. Adv. Prep. Conj. Int. | | | | | | | | fireman | | the | has rushed | | into | and | hurrah house | | that | | | up | and | stairs | | cool | | | | | | | | fearless | | | | | | | burning | | | | |

+Oral Parsing+ of the *conjunction* and the *interjection*.

The two *ands* are conjunctions, because they *connect*. The first connects two word modifiers; the second, two phrase modifiers. *Hurrah* is an *interjection*, because it expresses a burst of sudden feeling.

1. The small but courageous band was finally overpowered. 2. Lightning and electricity were identified by Franklin. 3. A complete success or an entire failure was anticipated. 4. Good men and bad men are found in all communities. 5. Vapors rise from the ocean and fall upon the land. 6. The Revolutionary war began at Lexington and ended at Yorktown. 7. Alas! all hope has fled. 8. Ah! I am surprised at the news. 9. Oh! we shall certainly drown. 10. Pshaw! you are dreaming. 11. Hurrah! the field is won.

LESSON 37.

PUNCTUATION AND CAPITAL LETTERS.

+COMMA—RULE.—Phrases that are placed out of their natural order [Footnote: A phrase in its natural order follows the word it modifies.] and made emphatic, or that are loosely connected with the rest of the sentence, should be set off by the comma+.

PUNCTUATE THE FOLLOWING SENTENCES.

+Model+.—The cable, *after many failures,* was successfully laid. Upon the platform 'twixt eleven and twelve I'll visit you. To me this place is endeared by many associations. Your answers with few exceptions have been correctly given. In English much depends on the placing of phrases.

+COMMA—RULE.—Words or phrases connected by conjunctions are separated from each other by the comma unless all the conjunctions are expressed+.

PUNCTUATE THE FOLLOWING SENTENCES.

+Model+.—Caesar *came, saw, and conquered.*
     Caesar *came and saw and conquered.*

He travelled in *England, in Scotland, and in Ireland.*

(The comma is used in the first sentence, because a conjunction is omitted; but not in the second, as all the conjunctions are expressed.)

A brave prudent and honorable man was chosen.

Augustus Tiberius Nero and Vespasian were Roman emperors.

Through rainy weather across a wild country over muddy roads after a long ride we came to the end of our journey.

+PERIOD and CAPITAL LETTER—RULE.—*Abbreviations* generally begin with capital letters and are always followed by the period+.

CORRECT THE FOLLOWING ERRORS.
+Model.—+*Mr., Esq., N. Y., P. M.*

gen, a m, mrs, no, u s a, n e, eng, p o, rev, prof, dr, gram, capt, coi, co, va, conn.

+EXCLAMATION POINT—RULE.—All *exclamatory expressions* must be followed by the exclamation point+.

PUNCTUATE THE FOLLOWING EXPRESSIONS.

+Model.—+*Ah! Oh! Zounds! Stop pinching!*

Pshaw, whew, alas, ho Tom, halloo Sir, good-bye, welcome.

Printed by BoD™in Norderstedt, Germany